CONTENTS

DIVA

Torrie®

Height: 5-foot-7
From: Boise, Idaho
Signature Move: Springboard Elbow

Torrie Wilson has been one of the hottest Divas in WWE since her debut in 2001. Torrie began her caree[r] in WCW where she worked with some of the WCW's biggest stars, including Ric Flair and Rey Mysterio. When Mr. McMahon bought WCW in 2001, it would not be long before Torrie signed a deal to work for WWE. Soon afte[r] joining WWE, Torrie aligned herself with other former WCW and ECW employees in a group known as "The Alliance". "The Alliance" became involved in a bitter rivalry with WWE Superstars. The group would eventually lose the battle and b[e] forced to leave their WCW pasts behind.

The next step in Torrie's journey came when she managed "The Japanese Buzzsaw" Tajiri. Tajiri did not allow Torrie to show off her considerable assets to the WWE fans, forcing Torrie to eventually rebel and become a firm fan favourite.

In 2003, Torrie Wilson graced the cover of the men's magazine *Playboy*, and became one of the most recognisable women in the world. Torrie may not have ever been a Women's Champion, but she does hold one major distinction. She participated in the most-purchased match on WWE 24/7 Online, a Bikini Contest against Sable at *Judgment Day 2002*. Not only were Torrie and Sable decked out in two of the hottest bikinis ever seen, but they also sealed the match with a kiss that has to be seen to be believed.

GREATEST HITS...

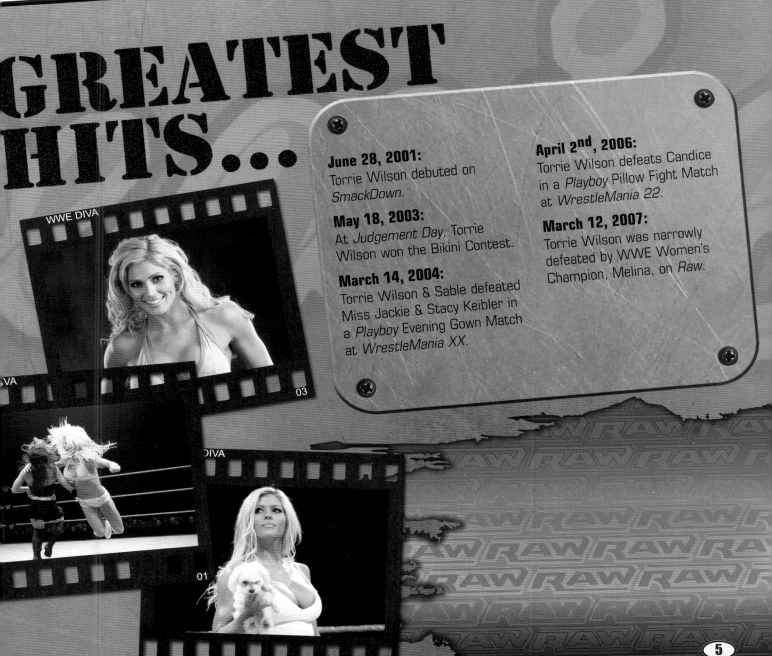

WWE DIVA

June 28, 2001:
Torrie Wilson debuted on *SmackDown*.

May 18, 2003:
At *Judgement Day*, Torrie Wilson won the Bikini Contest.

March 14, 2004:
Torrie Wilson & Sable defeated Miss Jackie & Stacy Keibler in a *Playboy* Evening Gown Match at *WrestleMania XX*.

April 2nd, 2006:
Torrie Wilson defeats Candice in a *Playboy* Pillow Fight Match at *WrestleMania 22*.

March 12, 2007:
Torrie Wilson was narrowly defeated by WWE Women's Champion, Melina, on *Raw*.

Melina ™

From: Los Angeles, CA
Associates: Johnny Nitro
WWE Debut: April 2005

Born in Los Angeles, Melina began her career as a fashion model. Upon encouragement from friends, she signed on with the WWE's reality show, *Tough Enough III*. Shortly thereafter she aligned herself with Johnny Nitro, and the two have been inseparable ever since. Melina, Nitro and Joey Mercury debuted on *SmackDown* in April 2005 as MNM and made an immediate impact, attacking Rey Mysterio on *Carlito's Cabana*. Just one week later, in their first official match on *SmackDown*, MNM defeated Eddie Guerrero and Rey Mysterio for the WWE Tag Team Championship.

Nitro & Melina made their *Raw* debut on May 29, 2006, but Nitro lost to John Cena after tapping out to the STFU. However, Nitro did manage to score his first *Raw* victory the following week when he defeated Charlie Haas, with some assistance from Melina.

Melina won her first WWE Women's Championship on February 19, 2007, just two weeks after her failed first attempt for the gold. With the paparazzi stationed at ringside, the loudest WWE Diva of them all took the title off her bitter rival Mickie James in a back and forth battle.

GREATEST HITS...

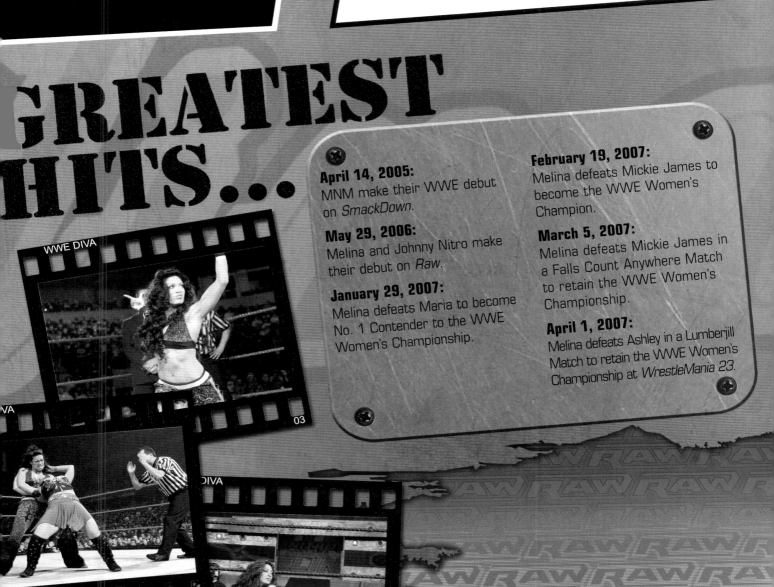

WWE DIVA

03

DIVA

01

April 14, 2005:
MNM make their WWE debut on *SmackDown*.

May 29, 2006:
Melina and Johnny Nitro make their debut on *Raw*.

January 29, 2007:
Melina defeats Maria to become No. 1 Contender to the WWE Women's Championship.

February 19, 2007:
Melina defeats Mickie James to become the WWE Women's Champion.

March 5, 2007:
Melina defeats Mickie James in a Falls Count Anywhere Match to retain the WWE Women's Championship.

April 1, 2007:
Melina defeats Ashley in a Lumberjill Match to retain the WWE Women's Championship at *WrestleMania 23*.

Mickie James ™

Height: 5-foot-4
From: Richmond, Va.
Career Highlights: Women's Champion

After Mickie James stormed onto the *Raw* scene in the fall of 2005, the WWE Divas division hasn't been the same. With an excitable attitude and a killer "Mick Kick," she ran into the ring on *Raw*, defending Trish Stratus against a vicious Victoria.

Soon after, James revealed that she idolised Trish, watching many of her matches with her "grandpappy." This desire to be aligned with one of her heroes would ultimately lead to a massive fallout between the two.

Stratus felt Mickie was too overbearing, and her eagerness to please often resulted in unfavourable outcomes. Trish finally told Mickie that enough was enough, and that they needed some space from each other. Afterward, Mickie explained that Trish broke her heart, and now she was going to break Trish.

The feelings of dejection boiled over into *WrestleMania 22* in Chicago, IL, where James proved that she knows exactly what she's doing inside the ring. Arguably, the best women's matchup ever for a *WrestleMania*, James hit Stratus with a series of hard blows followed by a Mick Kick to capture her first Women's Championship. With the raw skill and talent James possesses, she hopes to continue dominating the pack.

GREATEST HITS...

WWE DIVA

IVA

DIVA

01

03

October 10, 2005:
Mickie James debuts on *Raw*.

January 29, 2006:
Mickie James defeats Ashley at the *Royal Rumble*.

March 18, 2006:
Mickie James & Trish Stratus defeat Candice & Victoria at *Saturday Night's Main Event*.

April 2, 2006:
Mickie James defeats Trish Stratus for the WWE Women's Championship at *WrestleMania 22*.

June 7, 2006:
Mickie James defeats ECW's Jazz to retain the WWE Women's Championship.

November 26, 2006:
Mickie James defeats Lita to win her second WWE Women's Championship at *Survivor Series*.

ASHLEY

VS

MELINA

And here come the Lumberjills.

Look at all these Hot Divas...

Here comes the challenger, Ashley.

And she looks like she is ready for this match.

Here is the WWE Women's Champion, Melina.

I just love her entrance.

And the champ raises her belt high above her head!

Ashley is so fired up for this match!

Just look at Melina taunting the challenger Ashley with the championship belt.

Melina is showing great strength here, spinning Ashley round before slamming her to the ground.

And you know that landing had to hurt!

Melina with a blatant choke!

Melina looks like she is setting up Ashley for some sort of Surfboard manoeuvre.

Just look at the pain etched on Ashley's face.

Ashley really needs to escape from this predicament!

And she does! She has Melina set up for the flying head scissors!

And Ashley takes the champ down with that spectacular move!

Ashley hits Melina with a huge right hand!

Ashley goes to the top rope looking for a massive elbow drop!

But Melina rolls out of the way and rolls Ashley up for the pin!

16

The Lumberjills are invading the ring! It's an all out Diva war!

And doesn't she look happy about it!

Melina has retained the WWE Women's Championship!

Ashley™

Height: 5-foot-5
From: New York, NY
Signature Move: Starstruck
Career Highlights: Won the 2005 RAW Diva Search, *Playboy* Cover Girl.

Ashley grew up in Babylon, NY. Her father, brother and uncle were all amateur wrestlers and were the first to introduce the "Dirty Diva" to the world of sports-entertainment. Ashley enjoyed many sports while growing up. Possessing strong gymnastic and athletic capabilities, Ashley applied for the 2005 WWE Diva Search. Her mix of athleticism, spunk and beauty struck a chord with WWE fans, which supported her throughout the contest. In the finals, Ashley made a bold move, giving fans her cell phone number live on Raw and asking for their support. The voters were cast, and Ashley scored a resounding victory to earn a WWE contract.

At *WrestleMania 23*, Ashley was narrowly defeated by WWE Women's Champion Melina in a Lumberjill Match featuring nearly every WWE Diva on the WWE roster. But Ashley served notice to all at Ford Field that day and the millions watching on pay-per-view: She will be a major force for a long time to come in WWE.

GREATEST HITS...

August 15, 2005:
Ashley is announced as the winner of the 2005 Raw Diva Search.

January 8, 2006:
Ashley defeats Maria, Candice, Torrie Wilson and Victoria in a Bra & Panties Gauntlet Match at *New Year's Revolution*.

July 23, 2006
Ashley defeats Kristal, Jillian Hall and Michelle McCool at *The Great American Bash*.

WWE DIVA

03

DIVA

01

Candice ™

From: Milwaukee, Wis.
Career Highlights: Playboy cover girl
Associates: Victoria

Becoming one of the most recognisable WWE Divas of all time, Candice has been heating things up inside the ring since her *Raw* debut in 2004.

But Candice's star is rising even higher. The devilis Diva was the cover girl for the April 2006 edition of *Playboy*. Bearing all, Candice is following in the footsteps of other WWE Divas such as Torrie Wilson, Sable and Chyna. But, according to Candice, she is th hottest Diva to ever grace the cover of the popular men's magazine.

She drove this point home on the March 6, 2006 edition of *Raw*. Torrie Wilson and Victoria helped Candice unveil her red-hot cover. After the cover was revealed, Candice took a shot at Torrie, claiming that she was hotter in *Playboy* than Wilson was. Torrie took offence and let Candice know. The two embraced, giving the appearance that all was forgiven. But Candice signalled to Victoria with a wink, and the two double-teamed Torrie. Candice's beauty is only matched by her devious mean streak.

In addition to starring in a couple of commercials for GoDaddy.com, Candice also put in a bid to become *Raw's* newest general manager. Only Candice knows what her next goal will be. But one thing is for sure. She'll do whatever it takes to get the job done.

GREATEST HITS...

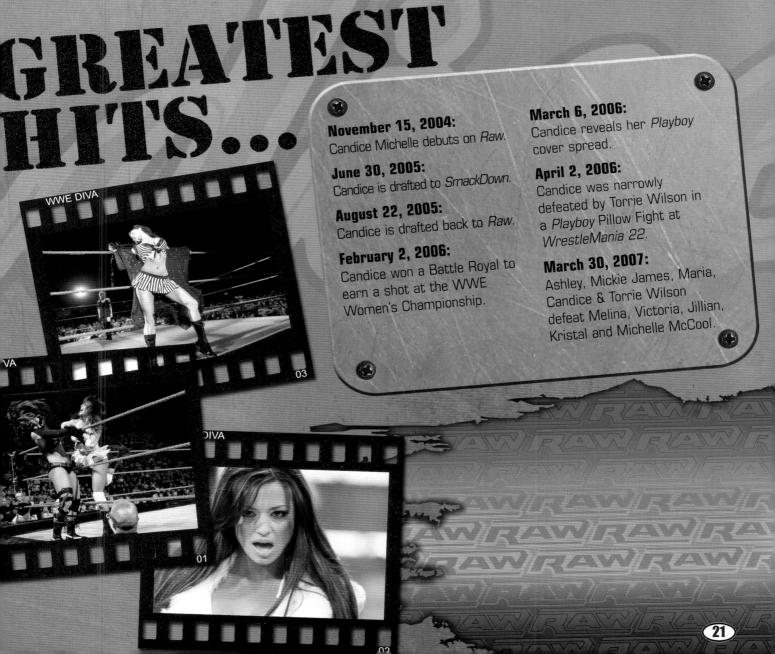

WWE DIVA

VA

DIVA

November 15, 2004:
Candice Michelle debuts on *Raw*.

June 30, 2005:
Candice is drafted to *SmackDown*.

August 22, 2005:
Candice is drafted back to *Raw*.

February 2, 2006:
Candice won a Battle Royal to earn a shot at the WWE Women's Championship.

March 6, 2006:
Candice reveals her *Playboy* cover spread.

April 2, 2006:
Candice was narrowly defeated by Torrie Wilson in a *Playboy* Pillow Fight at *WrestleMania 22*.

March 30, 2007:
Ashley, Mickie James, Maria, Candice & Torrie Wilson defeat Melina, Victoria, Jillian, Kristal and Michelle McCool.

Michelle McCool ™

Height: 5-foot-10
From: Palatka, Fla.

In August 2004, Michelle McCool was eliminated from the 2004 Raw Diva Search competition, but that would not be the last WWE fans would see of this disciplinary Diva. On November 18, 2004, McCool returned to *SmackDown*.

In the summer of 2006, however, McCool's attitude started to change. She became much stricter, much more business-like and warned all the other Divas that she was "going to take them to school."

A former schoolteacher, Michelle McCool is one of *SmackDown*'s most studious of Divas. The stunningly beautiful and athletic McCool is a woman of many skills, gets into the ring to mix it up with the rest of the Divas on a weekly basis.

GREATEST HITS...

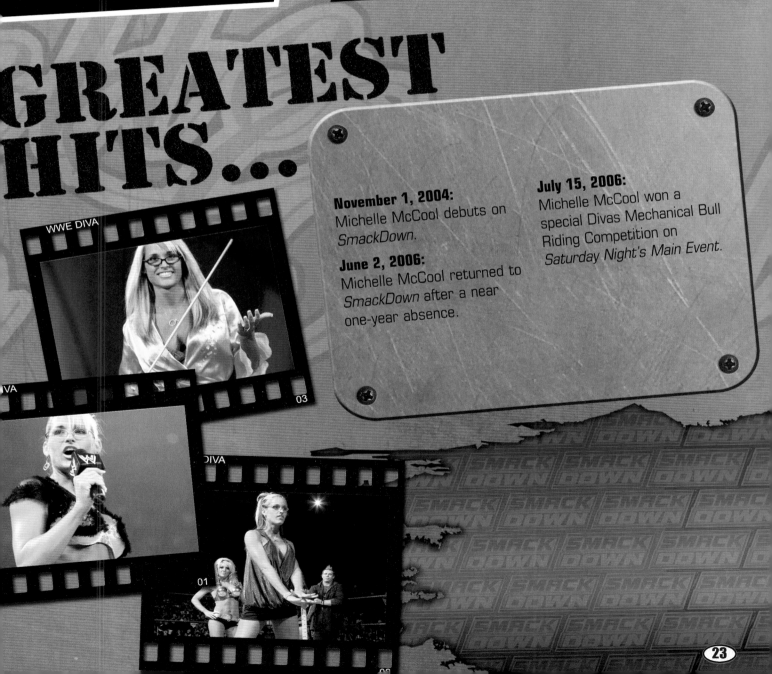

WWE DIVA

IVA

03

November 1, 2004:
Michelle McCool debuts on *SmackDown*.

June 2, 2006:
Michelle McCool returned to *SmackDown* after a near one-year absence.

July 15, 2006:
Michelle McCool won a special Divas Mechanical Bull Riding Competition on *Saturday Night's Main Event*.

DIVA

01

Diva Quiz

Q1.

Which ECW Diva is known as a "Full Bodied Italian"?

A. Layla	☐
B. Trinity	☐
C. Kelly Kelly	☐

Q2.

Who did Ashley face for the WWE Women's Championship at *WrestleMania 23*?

A. Mickie James	☐
B. Candice	☐
C. Melina	☐

Q3.

Which two Divas have been merged together in this picture?

A. Melina and Ashley	☐
B. Layla and Ashley	☐
C. Mickey James and Melina	☐

Q4.

Where was Lilian Garcia born?

A. Madrid, Spain	☐
B. London, England	☐
C. Paris, France	☐

Q5.

Which Diva wears this ring attire?

A. Maria	☐
B. Queen Sharmell	☐
C. Ashley	☐

Q6.

Which Divas entrance music contains the line "I ain't a woman to mess with!"?

A. Victoria ☐

B. Maryse ☐

C. Torrie ☐

Q7.

Who did Melina defeat for her first WWE Women's Championship?

A. Ashley ☐

B. Michelle McCool ☐

C. Mickie James ☐

Q8.

How many times has Mickie James been WWE Women's Champion?

A. Once ☐

B. Twice ☐

C. Three Times ☐

Q9.

Can you identify this Diva from just her eyes?

A. Maria ☐

B. Trinity ☐

C. Layla ☐

Q10.

In which year was Torrie Wilson crowned Miss Galaxy?

A. 2005 ☐

B. 1998 ☐

C. 2000 ☐

Diva Quiz

Score

/10

Add up your score...

Diva Quiz

CAN YOU IDENTIFY ALL OF THESE HOT WWE DIVAS FROM JUST THESE PHOTOS?

B.

C.

A.

D

E.

F.

G.

H.

Diva Quiz

Score

/8

Add up your score...

Victoria ™

From: San Bernardino, Calif.
Signature Move: Widow's Peak
Career Highlights: Women's Champion

Victoria is one of the most vicious Divas in WWE history. Don't let her impeccable good looks fool you. She may be one of the hottest Divas around, but Victoria's beauty is only matched by a mean streak that has helped drive her to two Women's Championships.

Armed with one of the most devastating finishing manoeuvres in all of WWE, the Widow's Peak, Victoria had recently aligned herself with two other Divas, Torrie Wilson and Candice. Being the most accomplished competitor of the three, Victoria was often looked upon to fill the enforcer role of the trio, but it was a role she gladly accepted.

Victoria made her WWE debut in 2002 and has been a top-flight women's competitor ever since. She has held the WWE Women's Championship twice, defeating Trish Stratus at *Survivor Series* in 2002 and then getting the better of Molly Holly, Jazz and Lita on an episode of *Raw* in February 2004. She remains to this day a contender for the title and a competitor that all the other WWE Divas should look out for.

GREATEST HITS...

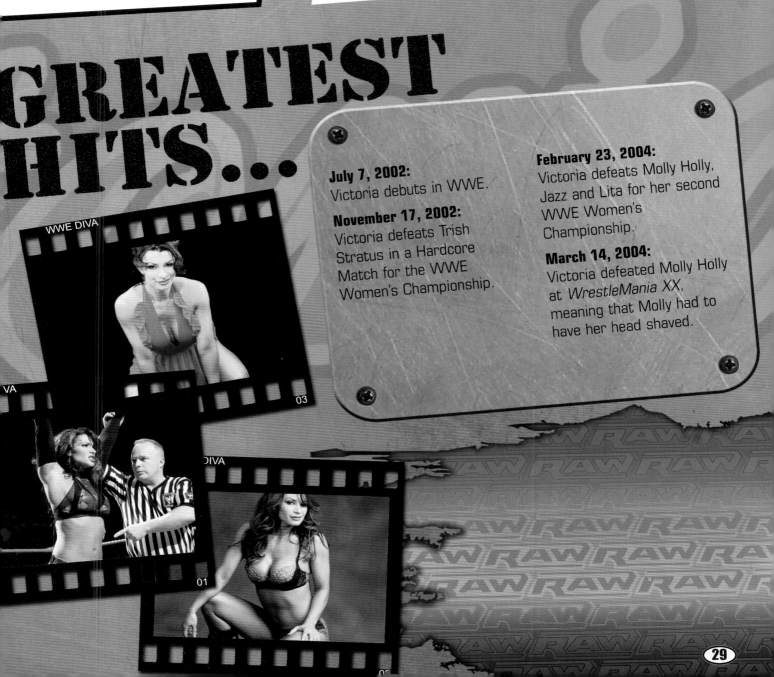

July 7, 2002:
Victoria debuts in WWE.

November 17, 2002:
Victoria defeats Trish Stratus in a Hardcore Match for the WWE Women's Championship.

February 23, 2004:
Victoria defeats Molly Holly, Jazz and Lita for her second WWE Women's Championship.

March 14, 2004:
Victoria defeated Molly Holly at *WrestleMania XX*, meaning that Molly had to have her head shaved.

WWE DIVA

VA

DIVA

03

01

Kelly Kelly ™

Career Highlights: Performs "Kelly's Exposé" on *ECW* on *Sci Fi*

Associates: Layla and Brooke (Extreme Exposé)

When she debuted on June 13, Kelly Kelly became the youngest diva in all of sports-entertainment. A self-proclaimed exhibitionist, she put on burlesque shows dubbed "Kelly Kelly's Exposé" for ECW fans and won several body competitions. Unfortunately for Kelly, her boyfriend, Mike Knox, insisted that she cover up.

n Knox's corner, Kelly earned her
ECW stripes, taking cane shots from
Sandman for her boyfriend. Perhaps
his is why Kelly' eyes have begun to
wander from her current boyfriend,
as Kelly has exposed not just her
body, but also her love for CM Punk.

Most recently, Kelly has teamed with
fellow ECW Divas Layla and Brooke
to entertain the crowd with their
unforgettable dance routines.

GREATEST
HITS...

May 2006:
Kelly Kelly signs with WWE.

June 13, 2006:
Kelly Kelly debuts on ECW.

December 5, 2006:
Kelly Kelly defeats Ariel in a
major upset on ECW.

January 28, 2007:
Kelly Kelly was responsible for
handing out the entry numbers
for the *Royal Rumble*.

February 18, 2007:
Extreme Exposé took part in
a Diva Talent Contest at
No Way Out.

April 1, 2007:
Extreme Exposé were seen
dancing backstage with Cryme
Tyme at *WrestleMania 23*.

WWE DIVA

03

DIVA

01

Jillian™

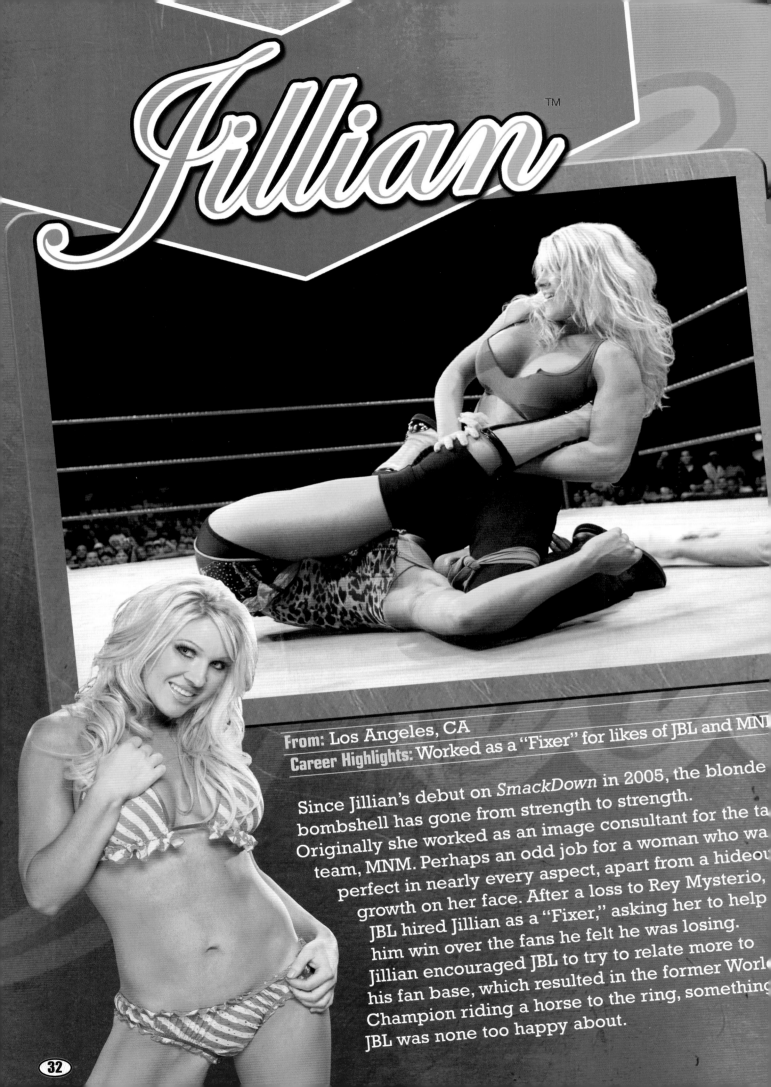

From: Los Angeles, CA
Career Highlights: Worked as a "Fixer" for likes of JBL and MN[M]

Since Jillian's debut on *SmackDown* in 2005, the blonde bombshell has gone from strength to strength. Originally she worked as an image consultant for the ta[g] team, MNM. Perhaps an odd job for a woman who wa[s] perfect in nearly every aspect, apart from a hideou[s] growth on her face. After a loss to Rey Mysterio, JBL hired Jillian as a "Fixer," asking her to help him win over the fans he felt he was losing. Jillian encouraged JBL to try to relate more to his fan base, which resulted in the former Worl[d] Champion riding a horse to the ring, something JBL was none too happy about.

While working for JBL, Jillian had a run in with the strangest Superstar to ever appear on *SmackDown*, The Boogeyman. During an episode of *Piper's Pit*, the legendary "Rowdy" Roddy Piper invited JBL, Jillian and Bogeyman to be his guests. Boogeyman chased JBL out of the ring and with no one to protect her, Jillian fell foul to the most disgusting case of "do it yourself" plastic surgery ever seen in the WWE as Boogeyman bit off her mole and chewed it up!

Shortly after Boogeyman's attack, Jillian was fired by JBL. Since then, her confidence has grown and she now loves to entertain her fans by singing in front of them whenever she has the chance. Jillian Hall has become a force in the *SmackDown* women's division. The stunning blonde relies on a broad arsenal of offensive tactics to overwhelm her opponents, and record countless victories.

GREATEST HITS...

WWE DIVA

DIVA

July 28, 2005:
Jillian debuts on *SmackDown* as MNM's image consultant.

September 16, 2005:
Jillian is hired by JBL as his "Fixer."

January 13, 2006:
Jillian has her facial growth bitten off by The Boogeyman.

April 21, 2006:
Jillian is fired by JBL.

May 21, 2005:
Jillian defeats Melina at *Judgment Day 2006*.

Lilian Garcia ™

From: New York, N.Y.
Career Highlights: *Monday Night Raw* ring announcer.

Lilian Garcia is perhaps best known as the ring announcer on *Monday Night Raw*, but this stunningly beautiful Diva has another talent that you may not be as familiar with. Lilian was singing from a very early age. When she and her family relocated to Columbus SC, she carried on developing her talent in high school choirs. By her early teens, she was being chaperoned by her mother as she worked in local clubs and bars as the lead singer of a band. Garcia went on to graduate cum laude from the University of South Carolina.

Lilian's first single, *Shout*, became a hit in the U.S. and she continues to work on various pop/rock projects. In November 2001, she even got to sing to New York City as she belted out some of her own songs on the WWE float in the Macy's Thanksgiving Day Parade.

She made WWE history by becoming the first female to announce at a *WrestleMania*, at *WrestleMania 22*. She has sung the national anthem in front of U.S. troops in Afghanistan and in Iraq and was the ring announcer for *WrestleMania 23*, the biggest *WrestleMania* yet! She has even lent her vocal talent to other WWE Superstars and Divas, in fact she can be heard on Victoria's entrance music.

GREATEST HITS....

WWE DIVA

03

August 1999:
Lilian Garcia makes her WWE debut.

August 26, 2002:
Lilian defeats Howard Finkel in an Evening Gown vs. Tuxedo Match to win the right to be *Raw's* ring announcer.

May 26, 2003:
Lilian sings "America The Beautiful" to celebrate Memorial Day and then shares some beers with Stone Cold Steve Austin.

December 23, 2004:
Lilian Garcia joins the *SmackDown* crew on their tour of Iraq.

December 19, 2005:
Lilian has the honour of singing "The Star Spangled Banner" for the troops in Afghanistan.

April 1, 2007:
Lilian acts as the ring announcer for *WrestleMania 23*.

DIVA

01

MICKIE JAMES VS VICTORIA
NEW YEARS REVOLUTION

Well here we are about to witness Mickie James defending her WWE Women's Championship against Victoria.

And there's the champ! The beautiful, Mickie James!

There you see the list of Victoria's victims from over the last few weeks.

☑ Candice Michelle
☑ Maria
☑ Torrie
☑ Mickie James
Women's Championship

The match is underway and Victoria goes straight to work on the champion with a painful looking submission hold!

Victoria wringing Mickie James' arm, but the champion counters with a cartwheel.

The challenger regains control with a side headlock to the champion.

Mickie James really needs to escape from this hold!

Mickie hits Victoria with a huge Armdrag which takes the challenger down.

And Mickie follows up with a devastating Dropkick!

Victoria is showing her vicious side her as she chokes Mickie on the middle rope!

And follows up with another great deep Armdrag.

Mickie battles back and hits Victoria with a great Clothesline!

Victoria looks like she my be setting Mickie up for the Widows Peak... But Mickie reverses it and hits Victoria with a Tornado DDT! 1...2...3! It's over!

Mickie James defeats Victoria and retains her title here at *New Years Revolution*!

NO WAY OUT
DIVA TALENT CONTEST

Well here we are Mizfits at *No Way Out*! Are you ready for the first Diva Invitational Talent Contest? OK! Let's get things underway with ECW's Extreme Exposé!

Brooke, Layla and Kelly Kelly really know how to strut their stuff in that ring!

I just can't get enough of these three girls, they're just so hot!

And hey! There's Kelly Kelly! She is one of ECW's most popular Superstars, and it's easy to see why!

There you see Brooke, and wow! She is looking great tonight, just like she does every night!

Well Mizfits, that is it for Extreme Exposé! What did you think?

And next up we have *SmackDown's* very own, Jillian Hall!

Extreme Exposé certainly don't look to pleased to be seeing Jillian this evening!

Wow! Jillian really isn't winning any fans here tonight!

None of you other Diva's are nearly as talented as me! I'm a pop superstar!

Oh no Mizfits! I think she is going to sing for us!

Please won't someone make it stop!

Thank God! It's Ashley making her way to ringside! She is getting the best reaction of the night!

As judge of this competition, I declare Ashley to be the winner of the Diva Invitational Talent Contest!

Well Mizfits! It's turned into a free for all here at *No Way Out*! It's all out Diva warfare!

Layla™

From: Miami, Fla.
Career Highlights: Winner of the 2006 $250,000 Diva Search
Associates: Kelly Kelly and Brooke (Extreme Exposé)

Layla El, the winner of the 2006 $250,000 Diva Search, was born in London and lives in Miami. Before becoming a spunky *SmackDown* Diva, she was a dancer for NBA basketball team Miami Heat, and performed with Kanye West during the MTV Video Music Awards. Layla has taken her hot dance steps to ECW, where along with Kelly Kelly and Brooke, she drops the jaws of ECW fans in Extreme Exposé.

During the Diva Search contest, Layla won immunity at Sgt. Slaughter's Diva Boot Camp obstacle course and she wowed the crowd with her dance moves to clinch the *Diva Search Talent Show*. *SummerSlam 2006* marked her first appearance as a WWE Diva.

Although Layla has yet to prove herself in the ring, her incredible dance moves and love for the fans has made her into one of the most popular WWE Divas there is. Now that Layla is a firm fixture in the ECW locker room, it can only be a matter of time until this hot young lady decides it is time to move from pirouettes to piledrivers and really get involved in the ECW mix!

GREATEST HITS...

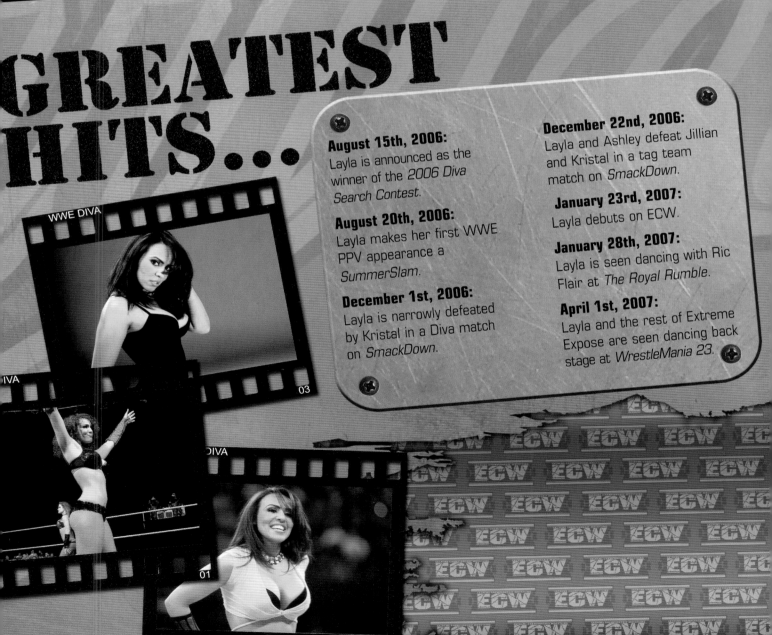

WWE DIVA

IVA

DIVA

03

01

August 15th, 2006:
Layla is announced as the winner of the *2006 Diva Search Contest*.

August 20th, 2006:
Layla makes her first WWE PPV appearance a *SummerSlam*.

December 1st, 2006:
Layla is narrowly defeated by Kristal in a Diva match on *SmackDown*.

December 22nd, 2006:
Layla and Ashley defeat Jillian and Kristal in a tag team match on *SmackDown*.

January 23rd, 2007:
Layla debuts on ECW.

January 28th, 2007:
Layla is seen dancing with Ric Flair at *The Royal Rumble*.

April 1st, 2007:
Layla and the rest of Extreme Expose are seen dancing back stage at *WrestleMania 23*.

Maria ™

From: Ottawa, Ill.
Career Highlights: Competed in the 2004 Raw Diva Search; Raw backstage interviewer.

Since Maria was 15, she has been involved in modelling, where she enjoyed much success. But it was WWE that the beauty had eyes for. Maria first captured the attention of WWE fans during the 2004 Raw Diva Search. Although she didn't win the competition, she continually impressed viewers. Soon after, she was signed by WWE as a locker room correspondent.

Shortly after beginning as a backstage interviewer, it became apparent that although Maria looked great on camera, sometimes her brain and her mouth didn't always work in harmony. Many memorable WWE moments have come from Maria's interviews. After Eugene & William Regal won the World Tag Team Championship, Eugene, excited and overwhelmed with the win, doused Maria with chocolate milk as part of the celebration.

Maria is also a featured attraction during WWE.com Unlimited segments during *Raw* commercial breaks. She often displays the latest WWE items up for auction, and she enjoys scanning the arena with her "Kiss Cam," leading to impromptu lip-locks between audience members.

GREATEST HITS...

November 1, 2004:
Maria debuts on *Raw* as a backstage interviewer.

December 19, 2005:
Maria & Candice defeat Trish Stratus & Ashley on *Raw Tribute to the Troops* from Afghanistan.

February 6, 2006:
Maria & John Cena defeat Edge & Lita with Maria scoring the pin!

October 16, 2006:
Maria defeated Torrie Wilson, Candice and Victoria in a Fatal Four-Way Match.

January 15, 2007:
Jeff Hardy & Maria defeat Johnny Nitro & Melina on *Raw*.

WWE DIVA

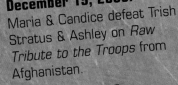

03

DIVA

01

Trinity ™

From: New York City
Signature Move: Moonsault
Associates: Little Guido Maritato

After working her way up through the ranks, Trinity was signed to WWE in late 2005. Just months later, she made her impact felt in a big way.

The "Full Bodied Italian" arrived in ECW and immediately turned heads. The sensuous Italian's outfit grabbed the attention of both ECW Superstars and fans alike.

Trinity soon found herself managing Little Guido Maritato, who has found her managerial services to be a large part of their offence. Could you concentrate on your opponents with Trinity distracting you at ringside? No I thought not!

But Trinity is just not another pretty face. She appears to be more than capable of mixing things up herself if the situation calls for it.

Without doubt, Trinity has some of the best in-ring skills of any WWE Diva, and it surely won't be long until she achieves championship gold, be it with her brain or with her brawn.

GREATEST HITS...

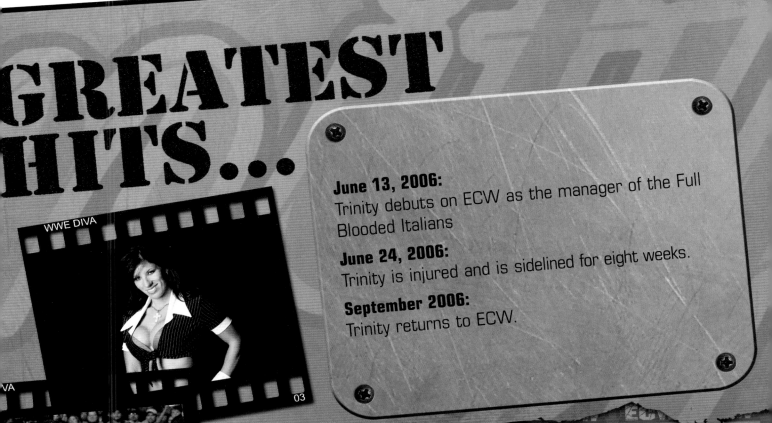

WWE DIVA

DIVA

03

01

June 13, 2006:
Trinity debuts on ECW as the manager of the Full Blooded Italians

June 24, 2006:
Trinity is injured and is sidelined for eight weeks.

September 2006:
Trinity returns to ECW.

Queen Sharmell ™

From: Houston
Career Highlights: 1991 Miss Black America
Associates: Booker T

Queen Sharmell got into the sports-entertainment business when she started working as a Nitro Girl in WCW. It was there that she met the man who would eventually, in March 2005, become her husband — Booker T. Shortly after their marriage, Sharmell started to accompany her man to the ring for his matches. It would not be long before Booker T's attitude started to change, largely due to Sharmell's influence. Booker went from being a fan favourite to becoming one of the most loathed Superstars in WWE today.

When Sharmell's interference helped Booker defeat Chris Benoit for the United States Championship in October 2005, the "Rabid Wolverine" questioned his friend about her involvement. The next week, Booker viciously attacked Benoit, revealing that he knew about Sharmell's involvement the whole time.

Things became even worse when Booker T defeated Bobby Lashley in the finals of the King Of The Ring Tournament and became the official King of *SmackDown*. King Booker made Sharmell his Queen, and the surreptitious Sharmell will now do anything it takes to help her King put royal gold around his waist.

Behind Sharmell's beautiful face is a devious mind, and she is not afraid to do whatever it takes to help her husband succeed on *SmackDown*.

GREATEST HITS...

WWE DIVA

IVA

DIVA

03

01

March 17, 2005:
Sharmell makes her WWE debut in the front row of the crowd cheering Booker T on during his match.

October 21, 2005:
Booker T defeats Chris Benoit for the United States Championship after Sharmell tripped Benoit from the outside of the ring.

May 21, 2006:
Booker T defeated Bobby Lashley in the finals of the King Of The Ring Tournament.

May 26, 2006:
King Booker had an official coronation ceremony and named Sharmell as his queen. Long live Queen Sharmell!

Diva Quiz

Q1.

Where was Lilian Garcia born?

A. Lisbon, Portugal ☐

B. Madrid, Spain ☐

C. Barcelona, Spain ☐

Q2.

Which two Divas are merged together in this picture?

A. Melina and Maria

B. Melina and Torrie ☐

C. Mickie James and Maria

Q3.

When Queen Sharmell worked for WCW as a Nitro Girl, what name did she use?

A. Chai ☐

B. Storm ☐

C. Saturn ☐

Q4.

Who did Victoria defeat to win her first Women's Championship

A. Lita

B. Trish Stratus ☐

C. Mickie James ☐

Q5.

Can you identify this Diva from just her eyes?

A. Melina ☐

B. Jillian ☐

C. Ashley ☐

52

Q6.

Which of these WWE Divas has never appeared in *Playboy*?

A. Ashley ☐

B. Torrie ☐

C. Kelly Kelly ☐

Q7.

In what year did Candice compete in the *Raw Diva Search*?

A. 2004 ☐

B. 2005 ☐

C. 2006 ☐

Q8.

Which WWE Diva wears this ring attire?

A. Torrie Wilson ☐

B. Lillian Garcia ☐

C. Mickie James ☐

Q10.

Who did Mickey James face at *New Years Revolution* in 2007?

A. Melina ☐

B. Candice ☐

C. Victoria ☐

Q9.

At which WWE PPV did Torrie face Candice in a *Playboy* Pillow Fight Match?

A. *The Great American Bash 2006* ☐

B. *No Way Out 2007* ☐

C. *WrestleMania 22* ☐

Diva Quiz

Score

/10

Add up your score...

SHARMELL

KELLY KELLY

TRINITY

Diva Links

HAVING YOUR VERY OWN DIVA AT RINGSI CAN BE A HUGE ADVANTAGE TO ANY WWE SUPERSTAR. CAN YOU MATCH WHIC DIVA GOES WITH WHICH WWE SUPERSTA

LONDON & KENDRICK

JOHNNY NITRO

CARLITO

MELINA

ASHLEY

TORRIE

MIKE KNOX

KING BOOKER

LITTLE GUIDO

Designer Divas

HAVE A GO AT DESIGNING A NEW OUTFIT FOR MELINA AND ASHLEY, AND SEE JUST HOW GOOD YOU CAN MAKE THEM LOOK...

Everyone knows that the WWE Divas are the hottest women on TV, but what you might not know is how hard these beautiful ladies have to work to look so good. It's not just all the working out, keeping their bodies in great shape, or all the wrestling training, honing their skills, looking for the chance to getting their shot at the gold, they also have to worry about what they are going to wear to the ring every night!

TRINITY

KELLY KELLY

AYLA

BROOKE

ECW
DIVAS

CANDICE

LILIAN GARCIA

MARIA

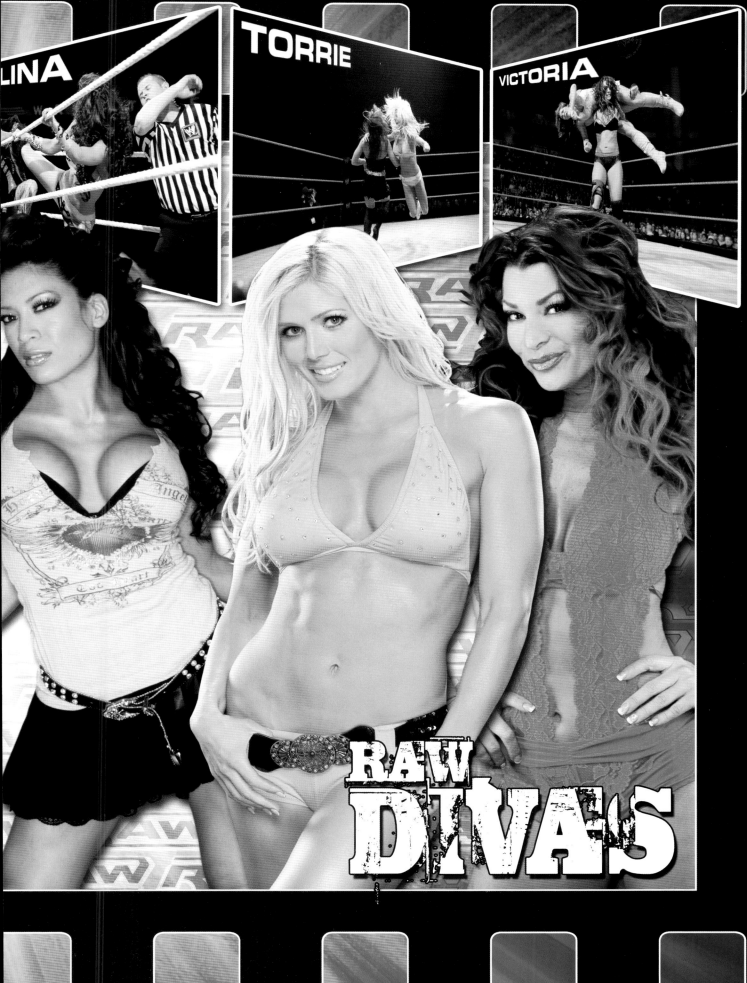

LINA

TORRIE

VICTORIA

RAW DIVAS

ASHLEY

KRISTAL

MICHELLE McCOOL